*Countries Around the World*

# Australia

Mary Colson

Heinemann Library
Chicago, Illinois

# www.capstonepub.com

Visit our website to find out more information about Heinemann-Raintree books.

# To order:

☎ Phone 888-454-2279

🖳 Visit www.capstonepub.com to browse our catalog and order online.

Edited by Catherine Veitch and Charlotte Guillain
Designed by Steve Mead
Original illustrations © Capstone Global Library Ltd 2012
Illustrated by Oxford Designers & Illustrators
Picture research by Hannah Taylor
Originated by Capstone Global Library Ltd
Printed in China by CTPS

15 14 13 12 11
10 9 8 7 6 5 4 3 2 1

Library of Congress Cataloging-in-Publication Data
Colson, Mary.
  Australia / Mary Colson.
    p. cm.—(Countries around the world)
  Includes bibliographical references and index.
  ISBN 978-1-4329-6094-0 (hb)—ISBN 978-1-4329-6120-6 (pb)  1.
Australia—Juvenile literature.  I. Title.
  DU96.C65 2012
  994—dc22                           2011015800

## Acknowledgments

We would like to thank the following for permission to reproduce photographs: Alamy Images p. 11 (© Photos 12); The Art Archive p. 7 (British Museum); The Bridgeman Art Library p. 8 (© Dixson Galleries, State Library of New South Wales); Corbis pp. 9 (Australian Picture Library/Cannon Collection), 20 (Specialist Stock), 29 (Jiang Yaping/Xinhua Press), 33 (©sylvain cazenave), 37 (Oliver Strewe); Dreamstime p. 18 (© Robert Gubiani); Getty Images pp. 16 (AFP/ William West), 32 (Scott Barbour); Istockphoto pp. 34 (© Ron Hohenhaus), 35 (© David Freund); © Ken Done p. 30; Photolibrary pp. 13 (age fotostock/San Rostro), 15 (Ticket/ Andrew Watson), 17 (Imagebroker.net/Michael Weber), 23 (Waterframe/Reinhard Dirscherl), 27 (Robert Harding Travel/ Ken Gillham), 31 (LOOK-foto/Hauke Dressler); Shutterstock pp. 5 (© Janelle Lugge), 6 (© Kharidehal Abhirama Ashwin), 19 (© twobluedogs), 21 (© Mogens Trolle), 24 (© Phillip Minnis).

Cover photograph of a tree and Ayers rock in the northern territory, Australia, reproduced with permission of Photolibrary (Ticket/ Jacob Halaska).

Every effort has been made to contact copyright holders of material reproduced in this book. Any omissions will be rectified in subsequent printings if notice is given to the publisher.

The author and publishers would like to thank Tim Dryden and Mairi Contos for their invaluable assistance in the preparation of this book.

# Contents

Some words in the book are in bold, **like this**. You can find out what they mean by looking in the glossary.

# Introducing Australia

What do you imagine when you think of Australia? Do you see kangaroos, crocodiles, and koalas? Or barbecues, surfers, and white, sandy beaches?

Australia is the world's largest island, with the Indian Ocean on one side and the Pacific Ocean on the other. It is one of the least populated countries in the world, with a huge wilderness in the center called the **outback**. The country is one-third desert, one-third semi-desert, and one-third fertile farmland. Much of the country's center is dry and waterless, but along the 16,007 miles (25,760 kilometers) of coastline, it is full of life.

It is a land of fragile rain forests, rugged coastlines, fertile valleys, tropical islands, and busy modern cities. It is also home to the largest living thing on Earth, the spectacular **Great Barrier Reef**.

## Unique and unusual

Australia's wildlife is **unique**. In 1780 the **naturalist** Joseph Banks sent a specimen of the duckbill platypus back to other naturalists in Great Britain. They did not believe that the strange-looking creature was real! Less funny are the country's deadly snakes, poisonous spiders, and fearsome sharks.

The country's **indigenous** people, the Aboriginals, have lived on the land for over 50,000 years. Europeans settled there just over 200 years ago. They named the land Terra Australis, which means "southern land" in Latin.

Australian inventors are responsible for the refrigerator, the ultrasound machine, and the electronic pacemaker. An Australian also invented Wi-Fi.

### How to say...

There are many indigenous languages in Australia. To say hello, the Arrernte people say *werte* (wurda). *Yaama* (yarma) is what the Gamilaraay people say, and the Pitjantjatjara people say *wai palya* (wa-ee palia).

Australia's dramatic landscape attracts
millions of visitors each year.

# History: Toward Equality

Aboriginals have lived in the country for tens of thousands of years. Human remains, thought to be about 40,000 years old, have been found at Lake Mungo, a dry lake in southeastern Australia. Aboriginals are believed to have sailed across the sea from the nearby countries of New Guinea and Timor. Over time, Aboriginals learned about the land, the creatures, and how to survive in harmony with nature.

## Daily life

Aboriginal tribes were hunter-gatherers, which means they moved around the country all year round in search of food. When they found food, they communicated with other groups by using a bullroarer. This is a flat piece of wood on a string that makes a whirring noise when it is spun. This noise can be heard across long distances.

Aboriginals used *woomera* (spear-throwers) and boomerangs to hunt for food.

By the 1600s, when European explorers arrived, there were around 350,000 Aboriginals living in about 250 different tribes. In each tribe, there were several **clans** with anywhere from 5 or 6 members up to as many as 30 or 40 members. Each tribe had its own language.

## European explorers

In 1642 the Dutch explorer Abel Tasman landed on the shores of what is now Tasmania, an island off the southeast coast of Australia. He named the island Van Diemen's Land, after Anthony van Diemen, his **patron**. Beginning in 1770, the British explorer James Cook sailed around Australia. He named many places, including Botany Bay.

The arrival of Europeans, who claimed the land for themselves, caused tensions with the **indigenous** people. It was not long before fighting broke out.

In Sydney Harbor in the 1700s, Aboriginals watch European ships arriving.

## Power shift

On January 26, 1788, the British claimed the east coast of Australia and raised a **Union Jack** flag in Sydney. Life changed dramatically for the Aboriginals. European diseases such as smallpox were deadly to them, because they had no resistance to these germs. A year later, a smallpox **epidemic** wiped out about 50 percent of the Aboriginals in the area. In 1803 Van Diemen's Land was **colonized** by the British as a **penal colony**. Prisoners were sent to Australia from Britain, often for crimes as minor as stealing a loaf of bread.

# WOOLLARAWARRE BENNELONG

## (AROUND 1764-1813)

Woollarawarre Bennelong was a member of the Eora, a tribe from the Sydney area. Bennelong served as an interpreter between the Eora and the British. He even traveled to Britain and met King George III.

Aboriginals tried to protect their lands from invasion. From the 1820s to the 1830s, war raged in Tasmania and other parts of Australia. Thousands of Aboriginal people were killed during fights with **settlers**. Their spears were no match for European guns, and they lost their lands.

# Gold rush!

In 1851 gold was discovered in the state of Victoria. The gold rush brought many **immigrants** to Australia from Europe, North America, and China. Victoria's population grew rapidly, from 77,000 in 1850, to 531,000 by 1858.

Miners work at the Angus Flat Goldmining Company mine at Forest Creek, Victoria, in 1857.

## Changing times

Between 1914 and 1918, over 400,000 Australian soldiers sailed to Europe to support Great Britain in World War I. Around 60,000 were killed, and a further 150,000 were wounded. Anzac (Australian and New Zealand Army Corps) soldiers fought at Gallipoli, in Turkey, where thousands died. Anzac soldiers also fought in World War II (1939–45), and in 2001 Australian troops were sent to fight in Afghanistan. All these soldiers are remembered on April 25, which is known as Anzac Day.

During the 1930s, the world **economy** failed, and the **Depression** years hit Australia hard. Its large wool and meat industries collapsed, causing mass unemployment and poverty.

## Social tensions

In 1992 Eddie Mabo won a court case giving land rights to indigenous people. The **Native** Title Act recognizes that Aboriginals owned the land first. It is a huge step toward correcting past wrongs.

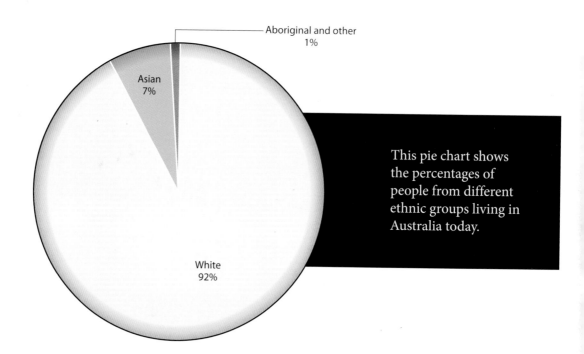

Aboriginal and other
1%

Asian
7%

White
92%

This pie chart shows the percentages of people from different ethnic groups living in Australia today.

## YOUNG PEOPLE

Between 1869 and 1969, the Australian government took many Aboriginal children away from their parents. They trained boys to become laborers and girls to become domestic helpers. These children, called the Stolen Generation, missed their parents and communities very much, and some tried to escape and find their way home.

Some progress toward **social equality** for indigenous people has been made. However, there are still challenges, such as equal education and work opportunities. In 2008 the Australian government finally apologized to Aboriginals for the suffering caused to the Stolen Generation (see box above). Over 100 years after the first children were taken from their families, the apology was an important moment in Australian history.

In this scene from the 2003 film *Follow the Rabbit-Proof Fence*, three Aboriginal children, who have been removed from their families, use a fence to find their way back home.

# Regions and Resources: Landscape and Living

Australia is a huge country of red deserts, dusty plains, and fertile farmland. Around one-third of the country is desert, the largest of which is the Great Victoria Desert, at 163,862 square miles (424,400 square kilometers). With a land area of 2,988,901 square miles (7,741,220 square kilometers), Australia is the sixth-largest country in the world. The population is over 21 million.

The country is mostly flat, but there are some mountain ranges. These include the Blue Mountains, the Snowy Mountains, and the Great Dividing Range, which runs the length of the east coast. Mount Kosciuszko is Australia's highest mountain, at 7,310 feet (2,228 meters).

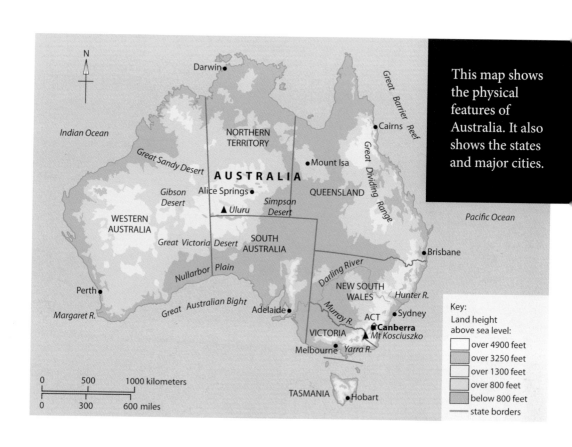

This map shows the physical features of Australia. It also shows the states and major cities.

Key:
Land height above sea level:
- over 4900 feet
- over 3250 feet
- over 1300 feet
- over 800 feet
- below 800 feet
- state borders

## Neighbors

Australia's nearest neighbor is Papua New Guinea, about 93 miles (150 kilometers) away. East Timor, Indonesia, and New Caledonia are the next-closest. New Zealand is about 1,000 miles (1,500 kilometers) to the southeast.

## Water sources

Australia's climate is dry in some areas and tropical in others. The town of Alice Springs, in the middle of the country, gets an average of 11 inches (28 centimeters) of rain per year. In contrast, the coastal city of Sydney gets 48 inches (121 centimeters) of rain per year. Most of the country's 22,780 square miles (59,000 square kilometers) of freshwater is used to **irrigate** land for farming. Large **desalination** plants along the coast turn seawater into freshwater.

## Special sites

Uluru is the world's largest **monolith** and is a **sacred** place for the Pitjantjatjara and Yankunytjatjara peoples. Some parts of Australia now belong to Aboriginal people. The largest and most famous is Arnhem Land. It is forbidden to enter these areas without a pass.

Uluru is 1,100 feet (348 meters) high and over 5.6 miles (9 kilometers) around.

## Land of plenty

Australia is divided into 6 states and 2 mainland territories, each with its own capital city. Canberra, in the southeast, is the capital city of the whole country. Western Australia has the largest area, at 965,255 square miles (2.5 million square kilometers). The city of Sydney, in New South Wales, has the largest population, with 4.5 million people. Around 89 percent of the population lives in cities along the coast.

## Farming focus

Agriculture is one of the most important industries in Australia and employs over 400,000 people. The dryer parts of the country, such as Western Australia, are mainly used for sheep and cattle grazing. Anna Creek Station, in South Australia, is the world's largest working cattle station, with just under 9,300 square miles (24,000 square kilometers) of land. Young people train on ranches to become jackaroos (cowboys) and jillaroos (cowgirls).

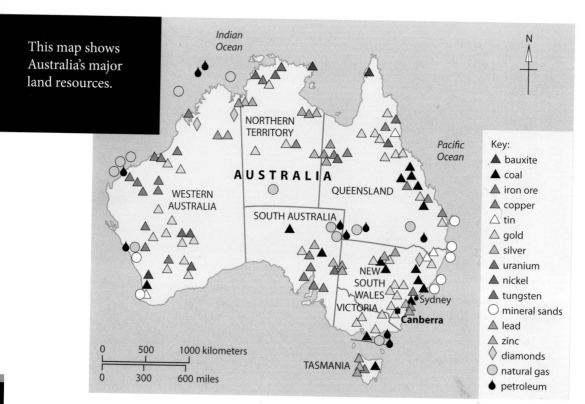

This map shows Australia's major land resources.

Key:
▲ bauxite
▲ coal
▲ iron ore
▲ copper
△ tin
△ gold
△ silver
▲ uranium
▲ nickel
▲ tungsten
○ mineral sands
△ lead
△ zinc
◇ diamonds
○ natural gas
◆ petroleum

Victoria and New South Wales get more rainfall and are the main **arable** states. In the tropical northern regions of Queensland and the Northern Territory, bananas, mangoes, oranges, and pineapples are grown.

## Mining matters

Over 120,000 people work in Australia's mining industry. The country has large reserves of gold, diamonds, copper, coal, and uranium. These mines are mostly in the **outback**. Australia provides more coal to other countries than any other place in the world. Famous mining towns include Broken Hill, Kalgoorlie, and Coober Pedy.

### Daily life

Many people in Coober Pedy work underground at the nearby opal mines. It gets so hot in the summer—around 122 °F (50 °C)—that much of the town is underground, including houses, stores, and the church. Visitors stay in an underground hostel to try to keep cool.

## Business matters

Australia has the 18th-largest **economy** in the world, worth around $889.6 billion each year. China is its biggest trading partner, followed by Japan, the United States, South Korea, India, and Thailand. The currency is the Australian dollar (A$). Instead of using paper money, Australia has plastic bills (banknotes), which are more difficult to **forge**. Australia has a workforce of 11.6 million people, and the average income is $39,900.

Australia has a developing high-tech economy. These medical scientists are carrying out research on cancer.

Most people live on the south and east coasts, so the main industries are concentrated there. There are many food processing factories, as well as chemical, steel, and manufacturing plants. **Biotechnology** companies carry out research into climate change and alternative energy sources. For a country with very low rainfall, this is key to its economic future.

## YOUNG PEOPLE

The Australian economy has coped extremely well with the global financial problems that began in 2007. Overall unemployment is very low, at 5.6 percent, but youth unemployment is very high. A quarter of young people between the ages of 20 and 24 are not working. The government is trying to help by providing extra training or work experience for young people.

Nearly six million tourists visit Australia every year.

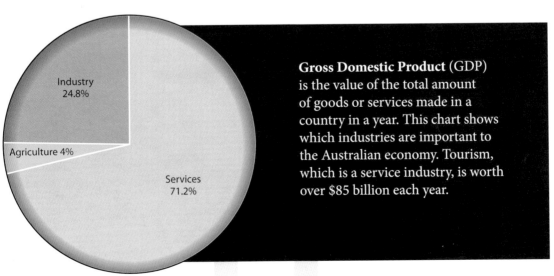

Industry
24.8%

Agriculture 4%

Services
71.2%

**Gross Domestic Product** (GDP) is the value of the total amount of goods or services made in a country in a year. This chart shows which industries are important to the Australian economy. Tourism, which is a service industry, is worth over $85 billion each year.

# Wildlife: Amazing Animals and Natural Wonders

Australia has some of the most unusual creatures and plants in the world. It also has many **introduced animals**, which harm the environment and put **native** animals at risk.

Marsupials have pouches in which they carry their young. Australia's most famous marsupial is the kangaroo, but there are many others. A relative of the kangaroo, the quokka, exists mainly on Rottnest Island, off the Western Australian coast. The wombat is a burrowing animal that has its pouch on its back. The koala eats eucalyptus leaves and sleeps for 18 hours a day.

The spiny echidna is a distant relative of the porcupine and is found throughout Australia.

## Introduced species

Rabbits, rats, and cane toads were introduced by early **settlers** and are now pests. The cane toad was brought in to protect the sugar cane crops of Queensland from beetles. Unfortunately, cane toads, rabbits, and rats reproduce quickly, eat **endangered** native animals and plants, and damage **habitats**.

## Watch out—camels crossing!

In 1860 Robert O'Hara Burke and William John Wills set out on an **expedition** across the middle of Australia. Camels were brought in to carry their equipment. Today, there are up to one million camels in Australia, many in wild herds.

### How to say...

Did you know that the names of some native Australian animals have come from Aboriginal languages? The koala, kangaroo, wombat, wallaby, barramundi, budgerigar, and kookaburra (a large kingfisher with a call that sounds like human laughter) are all Aboriginal words that have been adopted into the English language.

Road signs in the **outback** warn drivers to look out for animals crossing.

# Deadly beauty

The tropical waters around Australia are full of fantastic creatures, such as sharks, seahorses, and even sea dragons. Some of these amazing animals are also deadly.

At roughly 8 inches (20 centimeters) long, the beautiful blue-ringed octopus is a small creature, but it has one of the most **toxic venoms** in the world. When it is threatened, it turns an amazing electric blue color. Its venom can kill a human in minutes. There is no known **antidote** to the poison.

Box jellyfish glide around the coast. Their 31-inch- (80-centimeter-) long tentacles have poison on the tips. Jellyfish kill more people per year in Australia than snakes, sharks, and crocodiles.

Leafy sea dragons are protected by Australian law. They can grow up to 14 inches (35 centimeters) long.

## Crocs, snakes, and spiders

An adult male saltwater crocodile can be 20 feet (6 meters) long. They live in rivers in the tropical north of Australia. On average, saltwater crocodiles kill one person every year in Australia. In 2011 one lucky fisherman survived an attack by a 13-foot- (4-meter-) long crocodile by clinging on to mangroves on the riverbank and kicking his legs for 40 minutes until the croc gave up! Seven of the ten most poisonous snakes in the world live in Australia. The taipan has the most deadly venom, which can **paralyze** or even kill humans. The Red Back Spider, if disturbed, also delivers a poisonous bite to humans.

## Stinging trees

There are six different **species** of stinging tree in Australia. The most painful is the Gympie-Gympie. The sting comes from tiny hairs on its leaves and fruit. It can cause **cardiac arrest** in humans, but it is harmless to many native animals.

Saltwater crocodiles are excellent swimmers and have been spotted far out at sea.

# Managing the environment

Because it is a hot, mostly desert country, Australia faces many environmental challenges. Every year, wildfires rage out of control, destroying homes and livestock. Soil **erosion** caused by overgrazing cattle has left a lot of land unusable for growing crops. Australians are becoming increasingly aware of how to protect their environment, especially how to use water wisely.

## Daily life

All Australian states have water conservation procedures, which include sprinkler bans, bans on refilling swimming pools after use, and even rules about limiting washing machine use.

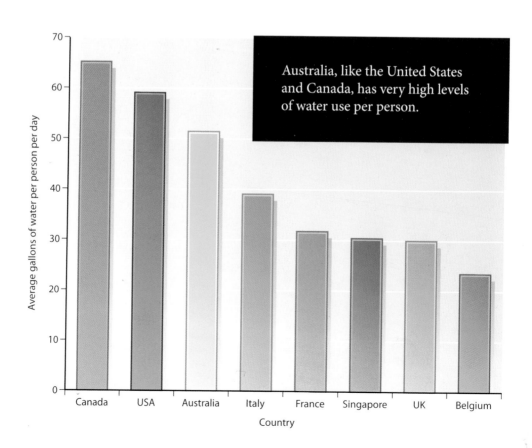

Australia, like the United States and Canada, has very high levels of water use per person.

# National parks

Australia has over 500 national parks and over 140 marine parks, covering an area of 233,205 square miles (604,000 square kilometers). Any development in the parks must be **sustainable**, and tourism is carefully controlled. The most famous park is the amazing **Great Barrier Reef**.

The reef is Australia's greatest natural wonder, at 1,864 miles (3,000 kilometers) long and 40 miles (65 kilometers) wide. A chain of more than 3,000 separate **coral** reefs, it is a spectacular sight, with more than 400 types of coral, 1,500 species of tropical fish, and over 20 types of **reptiles**, including sea turtles. Whales and dolphins are also found there. It is one of the world's most important, yet fragile, **ecosystems**. Millions of tourists visit the reef each year, but this can cause pollution and damage to the coral.

All visitors who enter Australia go through **biosecurity**. This is to prevent any foreign seeds or creatures from entering the country. Biosecurity protects the country's **unique** wildlife.

In order to protect the reef from pollution, the number of tourist boats on the reef is closely regulated.

# Infrastructure: Politics, Power, and People

On January 1, 1901, six independent British **colonies** on Australian soil agreed to join together. They became states of a new nation, the **Commonwealth** of Australia. Each state has its own government, which makes laws regarding education and development. The central government creates laws for the whole country and concentrates on the **economy** and defense.

## Two-tier system

The Australian government is divided into the Senate and the House of Representatives. Twelve senators from each state are elected every six years, along with two senators from each mainland territory. Elections for the 150 members of the House occur at least every three years. The main political parties are the Labor Party, Liberal Party, National Party, and Green Party.

The government is formed from the party with the largest number of votes. The prime minister is the leader of the government. The voting age is 18, and it is illegal not to vote. **Compulsory** voting was introduced in 1924 to increase participation in elections. People who do not vote can be fined.

The Australian parliament is in the capital city, Canberra.

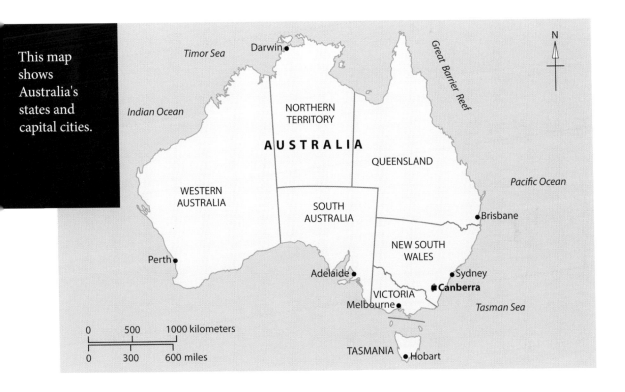

This map shows Australia's states and capital cities.

Timor Sea
Darwin
Indian Ocean
NORTHERN TERRITORY
AUSTRALIA
QUEENSLAND
Great Barrier Reef
Pacific Ocean
WESTERN AUSTRALIA
SOUTH AUSTRALIA
Brisbane
NEW SOUTH WALES
Perth
Adelaide
Sydney
Canberra
VICTORIA
Melbourne
Tasman Sea
0     500     1000 kilometers
0     300     600 miles
TASMANIA
Hobart
N

## JULIA GILLARD (BORN 1961)

In 2010 Julia Gillard became Australia's first female prime minister. Her family moved from Wales, a small country west of England, when she was four years old. She is the leader of the Australian Labor Party, as well as the head of government.

## Links with the United Kingdom

In 1942 Australia became independent of the United Kingdom and was able to create its own laws. But Australia remains part of the British Commonwealth, and the **head of state** is Britain's Queen Elizabeth II. Many Australians would like their country to become a **republic**, meaning the government is elected and there is no monarch (king or queen).

# Getting around

Australia's size means that traveling between cities is quicker by air than by road. The country has 326 airports with paved runways and many rough **landing strips** in the **outback**. There are 505,157 miles (812,972 kilometers) of roads, but only around 45 percent are paved. Highway 1 goes around the whole country. There are 1,243 miles (2,000 kilometers) of waterways, although these are mostly used for recreation rather than shipping.

# Trains on rails and roads

Major cities, such as Sydney, Melbourne, and Perth, have train networks. There are also railroads across the country. A train called the Indian Pacific goes from Perth to Sydney, and another called the Ghan goes from Adelaide to Darwin, through Alice Springs.

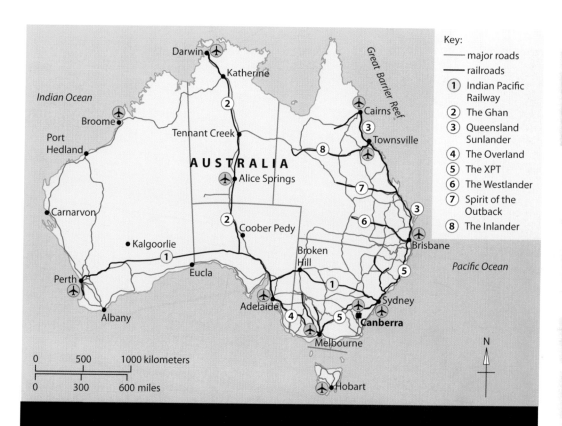

This map shows Australia's main road and railroad networks, as well as some major airports.

Australia also has special trucks they call "road trains." These travel across the middle of the country, carrying equipment and supplies. They are usually made up of an engine and three large trailers.

## Daily life

Every day, the Royal Flying Doctor Service saves lives across Australia's outback. Because the outback is so large, people who are sick cannot get to a hospital. So, they contact the Flying Doctors instead. A base in Alice Springs coordinates the calls and sends planes out from different airstrips.

The Royal Flying Doctor Service has been operating since 1928.

## School life

Australia's education system is made up of large schools in the cities and tiny schools on its islands and in the outback.

The school year runs from the end of January until mid-December, with a two-week winter break in July. There are four terms in the year, with a short vacation between each one. The school day usually begins at 9:00 a.m. and finishes around 3:30 p.m. Most children wear a uniform to school. Children go to kindergarten when they are five years old and continue on to secondary school when they are twelve.

Students study English, math, society and the environment, science, arts, foreign languages, technology, health, and physical education. Students also learn about Aboriginal culture. The government is aiming to provide all students in secondary school with laptop computers.

## Daily life

Some children in Australia cannot go to school because they live deep in the outback. Instead, they take classes by radio or online. Each morning, they "sign in" with their teacher, who tells them their lessons for the day. They check back in with the teacher if they have any questions or when they have completed the work.

## Community schools

In more far-off parts of the country, there are schools that put Aboriginal culture at the heart of the curriculum. Community schools are funded by the national government, but local committees decide what should be taught there. Aboriginal children have fewer educational opportunities than Australian children, and only 3 percent go on to further education such as college. Community schools and the government are working together to try to change this.

# YOUNG PEOPLE

Nearly 80 percent of Australian teenagers use the Internet most days, at both school and home. The average time spent online each week by 16-year-olds is around 23 hours.

Many Australian children use laptops every day at school.

# Culture: Art, Sports, and Food

Australian writers such as Miles Franklin, Kate Grenville, and Bryce Courtenay are celebrated storytellers. Aboriginals tell stories as part of their culture, too.

## Dreamtime

The Dreamtime is what Aboriginals call the beginning of the world. Their stories, art, and music explain different parts of the Dreamtime. Dreaming stories include how birds got their colors, why fish swim, and how **sacred** places were created.

Many Aboriginal artists paint Dreamtime images. These are usually made up of dots painted in bright colors. Other Australian artists, such as Margaret Preston, Brett Whiteley, Ken Done, and Sidney Nolan, are influenced by the sea, landscape, and light of the country.

## Design

Many of Australia's most recognizable types of clothing were designed to help people cope with the harsh conditions of farming life. The Driza-Bone coat is a long, waxy, waterproof coat, while Ugg boots have been worn by farmers in the **outback** for nearly 100 years.

This is Ken Done's painting of Sydney Harbor and the famous opera house.

## Entertainment

Australians love music, from the traditional Aboriginal didgeridoo sounds (see the photo below) to modern pop by stars such as Kylie Minogue. There are also many classical musicians, such as pianist Roger Woodward and conductor Richard Tognetti, who perform at the Sydney Opera House. Australia has produced world-famous actors, including Nicole Kidman, Cate Blanchett, Geoffrey Rush, Heath Ledger, and Hugh Jackman. Film director Baz Luhrmann is well known for his artistic movies.

### DAVID UNAIPON (1872–1967)

David Unaipon is known as the "Australian Leonardo." A member of the Ngarrindjeri people, he was a writer, a preacher, an artist, and an inventor. He is commemorated on the A$50 bill (banknote).

The didgeridoo is a traditional wooden wind instrument played by Aboriginals at festivals and celebrations.

# Sports

Australians are famous for their love of sports. The Australian way of life is centered around outdoor activities.

**Cricket** is a national sport. Horse racing, track and field, golf, and tennis are popular, too. The Melbourne Cup is a famous horse race that covers 1.9 miles (3.2 kilometers). Sydney hosted the Olympic Games in 2000. **Indigenous** athlete Cathy Freeman won the 400-meters gold medal. The Nullarbor Links, at 850 miles (1,365 kilometers) long, is the world's longest golf course. It takes players four days to finish. They have to drive across the dry and dusty Nullarbor Plain for a few hours between some of the holes! Tennis player Lleyton Hewitt has won two Grand Slam titles—Wimbledon and the U.S. Open.

## EVONNE GOOLAGONG (BORN 1951)

Evonne Goolagong is an Aboriginal tennis player. She won 13 Grand Slams, including four Australian Opens, two Wimbledon titles, and one French Open.

Over 100,000 people can watch cricket at the Melbourne Cricket Ground.

## Aussie rules

Australian rules football is very popular. Famous teams include Carlton and Hawthorn from Melbourne, the Sydney Swans, and the Brisbane Lions. Players can kick and pick up the oval-shaped ball, but if they run with it, they have to bounce it every few feet.

## Water sports

Most people live near the coast in Australia, so water sports and swimming are very popular. Swimmer Ian Thorpe has won five Olympic gold medals and is a national hero. There are over two and a half million surfers across the country and over 200 surfing events each year.

## LAYNE BEACHLEY
### (BORN 1972)

Layne Beachley became a professional surfer at the age of 16. In 1998 she became the Women's World Champion for the first time.

Layne Beachley won the World Championship title seven times.

## Food and drink

Australians love food, wine, and beer, and they have invented several dishes. Melba toast and Peach Melba both originated in Australia and were named after a famous opera singer, Dame Nelly Melba. One of the most famous Australian foods is a dark-brown paste called Vegemite, usually spread on bread or toast. In 1922 a chemist named C. P. Callister created Vegemite by using the leftovers from brewing beer.

### Daily life

Barbeques or "barbies" are an important part of Australian life. Most public parks have brick barbecues for people to use. Families take their own food and charcoal and spend the day together.

## Bush tucker

"Tucker" means "food," and "bush" means the "outback." So, "bush tucker" is food found in the wild. Aboriginals lived off bush tucker for thousands of years before Europeans arrived. Bush tucker guides do tasting tours of treats, such as sweet honey ants and slippery witchetty grubs. You can also try possum-tail soup and rooburgers in Australian restaurants.

Witchetty grubs live in the roots of witchetty trees. To find one, you have to dig into the roots of the tree.

# Lamingtons

Ask an adult to help you make this delicious treat.

**Ingredients for the cake**

- 3 eggs
- 1/2 cup sugar
- 1 1/4 cup self-rising flour
- 1/3 cup cornstarch
- 1 Tbsp melted butter
- 3 Tbsp hot water

**Ingredients for the chocolate icing**

- 5 cups powdered sugar
- 1 cup cocoa powder
- 1 Tbsp melted butter
- 1/2 cup milk
- 7 cups dried coconut

**What to do:**

1. Beat eggs and sugar together until blended. The sugar should dissolve.
2. Sift in the flour and cornstarch. Add the melted butter and hot water.
3. Pour the mixture into a square greased cake pan (7 x 11 inches).
4. Bake at 350 °F (180 °C) for about 30 minutes.
5. Flip the cake out onto a wire rack to cool before icing.
6. Sift the powdered sugar and cocoa into a bowl. Stir in the melted butter and milk.
7. Place the bowl over a pan of hot water and stir the mixture until the icing is shiny and runny.
8. Trim the brown top and sides from the cake. Cut it into square pieces.
9. Holding each piece with a fork, dip it into the icing.
10. Sprinkle the cake with coconut and place on a rack to set.

# Australia Today

Modern Australia is increasing its political status around the world and developing all the time. Australian society is multicultural and multi-faith, and it has a lively, **unique** culture. The Australian people are also becoming more aware of the environment. Flash flooding in Queensland in December 2010 ruined houses, destroyed crops, and took lives.

Australia's closest political **allies** are New Zealand, the United States, Japan, and the United Kingdom. Lots of young Australians want their country to be a **republic** and no longer connected to the British **Commonwealth**. But many older people want the British queen to remain their **head of state**.

## Official apology

There are still many social issues to resolve regarding the status of Aboriginals. Two organizations, the National Congress of Australia's First Peoples and Reconciliation Australia, work closely with the government to improve opportunities for Aboriginals. In 2010 Prime Minister Julia Gillard announced that Aboriginals should be recognized in the Constitution and that Australians would vote on this.

### MARY MACKILLOP (1842–1909)

In 2010 Australia celebrated the first of its citizens to be made a saint. Mary MacKillop was a Roman Catholic nun who devoted her life to helping and teaching children in the **outback**.

## How to say...

In the past, many Australians spoke in a special slang called "Strine." See if you can figure out what this sentence means: "Down Under, it's bonzer to go to the billabong and yabber away vegging out. Fair dinkum, you can fossick around all day, no dramas." The answer is at the bottom of the page!

Bondi Beach in Sydney is a popular place for families to spend time together and have fun.

Answer: In Australia, it's great to go to the lake to talk with friends and relax. Honestly, you can just hang around all day, with no worries.

# Fact File

| | |
|---|---|
| **Official language:** | English 78.5% |
| **Other languages:** | Chinese 2.5%; Italian 1.6%; Greek 1.3%; Arabic 1.2%; Vietnamese 1%; Other 8.2%; Unspecified 5.7% |
| **Currency:** | Australian dollar (A$). 100 cents make up the dollar. |
| **Capital city:** | Canberra |
| **Population:** | 21,766,711 (89% live in towns or cities) (July 2011 est.) |
| **Head of state:** | Queen Elizabeth II |
| **Religions:** | Christian 63.8%; Buddhist 2.1%; Muslim 1.7%; other 2.4%; unspecified, 11.3%; none 18.7% |
| **National colors:** | green and gold (most Australian sports teams use these colors in their uniforms) |
| **Life expectancy at birth:** | men—79.4 years; women—84.35 years |
| **Literacy rate:** | 99% of the population can read and write |
| **Climate:** | arid (dry) to semi-arid; temperate (mild) in south and east; tropical in north |
| **Natural resources:** | bauxite; coal; iron ore; copper; tin; gold; silver; uranium; nickel; tungsten; mineral sands; lead; zinc; diamonds; natural gas; petroleum |
| **Imports:** | machinery and transportation equipment; computers and office machines; crude oil and petroleum products |
| **Exports:** | coal; iron ore; gold; meat; wool; aluminum; wheat; machinery and transportation equipment |
| **Major industries:** | farming; mining;  tourism |
| **Natural hazards:** | **cyclones** along the coast; severe droughts (lack of rain); forest fires |
| **World Heritage Sites:** | 18, including Australian **Convict** Sites; Sydney Opera House; **Great Barrier Reef**; Greater Blue Mountains Area; Kakadu National Park; Tasmanian Wilderness; Uluru-Kata Tjuta National Park |
| **Major festivals:** | Sydney Festival; Ten Days on the Island (Tasmania); Dreaming Festival; Melbourne International Comedy Festival; Aboriginal Dance Festival; Adelaide Festival |

## Famous Australians

Ian Thorpe (swimmer), Shane Warne (**cricket** player), Cathy Freeman (athlete), Dr. Victor Chang (heart transplant surgery pioneer), Charles Edward Kingsford Smith (aviator), Kylie Minogue (singer), Bryce Courtenay (writer), Kate Grenville (writer), Arthur Boyd (artist), Margaret Preston (artist), Clifford Possum Tjapaltjarri (artist), Cate Blanchett (actor), Nicole Kidman (actor), Geoffrey Rush (actor), Rupert Murdoch (media boss)

## National holidays

| | |
|---|---|
| January 26 | Australia Day |
| April 25 | Anzac Day |
| June 14 | Queen Elizabeth II's birthday |

## National anthem: "Advance Australia Fair"

"Advance Australia Fair" is the national anthem of Australia. It was written in the 1800s by Peter Dodds McCormick. It was officially declared the national anthem on April 19, 1984. If a member of the British royal family is in Australia on an official visit, the British national anthem, "God Save the Queen," is also sung.

*Australians all let us rejoice,*
*For we are young and free;*
*We've golden soil and wealth for toil;*
*Our home is girt by sea;*
*Our land abounds in nature's gifts*
*Of beauty rich and rare;*
*In history's page, let every stage*
*Advance Australia Fair.*
*In joyful strains then let us sing,*
*Advance Australia Fair.*

# Timeline

BCE means "before the common era." When this appears after a date, it refers to the number of years before the Christian religion began. BCE dates are always counted backward.

CE means "common era." When this appears after a date, it refers to the time after the Christian religion began.

| | |
|---|---|
| about 50,000 BCE | Aboriginal people are thought to have reached Australia. |
| 40,000 BCE | Aboriginal engravings found in South Australia date back to this time. |
| 1642 CE | Dutch explorer Abel Tasman reaches Van Dieman's Land (now Tasmania). |
| 1770 | British explorer James Cook lands in Botany Bay. |
| 1788 | Britain claims the east coast of Australia. |
| 1803 | Van Dieman's Land becomes a British **colony**, and **convict** transportation begins. |
| 1820s–30s | War begins between Aboriginals and British **settlers** in Van Dieman's Land. |
| 1830 | Port Arthur opens as a **penal colony** in Van Dieman's Land. |
| 1851 | The gold rush begins in Victoria. |
| 1860–61 | Robert O'Hara Burke and William John Wills cross central Australia from south to north. |
| 1868 | The last convicts are transported to Australia. |
| 1869 | Aboriginal children begin to be removed from their families. |
| 1873 | Uluru is first visited by Europeans. |
| 1901 | Australia becomes a **commonwealth**, uniting all the states for the first time. |
| 1914–1918 | Australian troops fight in World War I. |
| 1922 | Vegemite is invented. |
| 1924 | **Compulsory** voting is introduced. |
| 1928 | The Royal Flying Doctors Service is established. |

| 1932 | Sydney Harbor Bridge opens. |
| 1939–1945 | Australian troops fight in World War II. |
| 1942 | Australia becomes independent of the United Kingdom, but retains the British queen as **head of state**. |
| 1956 | The Olympic Games are held in Melbourne. |
| 1971 | Neville Bonner becomes the first Aboriginal to be a member of parliament (the ruling body of the government where laws are made). |
| 1971 | Evonne Goolagong wins the first of her 13 total tennis Grand Slams. |
| 1973 | The Sydney Opera House opens. |
| 1984 | "Advance Australia Fair" becomes the national anthem. |
| 1992 | Eddie Mabo wins a court case giving Aboriginal people land rights. |
| 1996 | Geoffrey Rush wins an Oscar for Best Actor for his role in the movie *Shine*. |
| 1998 | Layne Beachley wins the women's world surfing championship for the first time. |
| 2000 | The Olympic Games are held in Sydney. |
| 2001 | Australian troops start serving in Afghanistan. |
| 2008 | Prime Minister Kevin Rudd formally apologizes to the Stolen Generation. |
| 2009 | The world's longest golf course, the Nullarbor Links, opens. |
| 2010 | Mary MacKillop becomes Australia's first saint. |
| 2010 | The Australian government announces a vote to change the Constitution to recognize Aboriginal people. |

# Glossary

**ally**  political partner

**antidote**  substance that acts against poison

**arable**  land suitable for growing crops

**biosecurity**  protecting a country or area from foreign plants or animals

**biotechnology**  energy or products created from plants or the natural world

**cardiac arrest**  heart attack

**clan**  small group of people, often closely related

**colonize**  when one country rules over another

**colony**  country ruled by another country

**commemorate**  remember something or somebody

**Commonwealth**  countries of the former British Empire

**compulsory**  when there is a requirement to do something

**convict**  person who has been found guilty of a crime

**coral**  type of living thing in the sea

**cricket**  bat and ball game played on an oval field; it is similar to baseball

**cyclone**  tropical storm

**Depression**  global economic crisis of 1930s

**desalination**  removing salt from seawater, to turn it into freshwater

**economy**  all the produce and trade of a country

**ecosystem**  group of plants and animals that depend on each other and share an environment

**endangered**  when animals or plants are at serious risk of dying out

**epidemic**  fast-spreading disease

**erosion**  wearing away of rock or land

**expedition**  organized journey or trip

**forge**  create illegal copies of something

**Great Barrier Reef**  world's largest system of coral reefs

**Gross Domestic Product** value of the total amount of goods or services made in a country, in a year

**habitat** place where plants or animals live

**head of state** person who is the chief representative of a country

**immigrant** person who comes to live permanently in a foreign country

**indigenous** coming from a particular place

**introduced animal** animal from elsewhere brought into a country for farming or other purposes

**irrigate** supply water to land and crops

**landing strip** rough runway in the countryside

**opal** gemstone

**outback** remote area; wilderness region

**monolith** block of solid stone standing by itself

**native** living in a place before anyone or anything else

**naturalist** person who studies the natural world

**paralyze** cause loss of movement due to nerve or muscle damage

**patron** person who gives financial or other support

**penal colony** place abroad where prisoners were sent

**reptile** cold-blooded, scaly animal that lays eggs

**republic** political system with an elected government and no king or queen

**sacred** holy

**settler** someone who moves to a country and settles there

**social equality** everybody having the same status and respect

**species** type of animal, bird, or fish

**sustainable** environmentally friendly way of using resources that avoids causing damage to the environment or harming supplies of resources

**toxic venom** poisonous fluid used by an animal to scare off predators

**Union Jack** flag of the United Kingdom

**unique** only one of its kind

# Find Out More

## Books

Allgor, Marie. *Endangered Animals of Australia* (*Save Earth's Animals!*). New York: PowerKids, 2011.

Bateman, Helen, and Jayne Denshire. *Australia* (*Famous Places of the World*). North Mankato, Minn.: Smart Apple Media, 2007.

Bingham, Jane. *Australia* (*Exploring Continents*). Chicago: Heinemann Library, 2007.

Scillian, Devin. *D Is for Down Under: An Australia Alphabet* (*Discover the World*). Ann Arbor, Mich.: Sleeping Bear, 2010.

Sheen, Barbara. *Foods of Australia* (*Taste of Culture*). Detroit: KidHaven, 2010.

Underwood, Deborah. *Australia, Hawaii, and the Pacific* (*World of Music*). Chicago: Heinemann Library, 2007.

## Websites

**http://australianmuseum.net.au/Stories-of-the-Dreaming/**
Enjoy stories of the Dreaming from different parts of Australia.

**http://kids.nationalgeographic.com/kids/places/find/australia/**
This website tells you more about Australia. Find out the basics about boomerangs and much more.

**www.australia.com**
This is the official national tourism website for Australia.

# Places to visit

If you are lucky enough to visit Australia, these are some of the places you could visit and activities you could try:

## Harbor Bridge climb, Sydney, New South Wales

Climb Sydney Harbor Bridge and get a bird's-eye view of the city, opera house, and port.

## Cape Tribulation rain forest, Queensland

Explore amazing rain forests and mangrove swamps and see tree kangaroos, crocodiles, and globe spiders.

## Great Barrier Reef, Queensland

Snorkel above the largest living thing on Earth. See the amazing colors and shapes of millions of fish and coral.

## Tall Timber Country, Western Australia

Walk among the treetops at this park and see the giant karri and tingle trees.

## Uluru, Northern Territory

Visit Australia's most famous rock. Take a guided tour around the sacred sites and see the amazing rock art. Watch Uluru change color as the sun sets.

## Australian Convict Sites, Tasmania

Around 166,000 male, female, and child prisoners were sent to Australia from Great Britain between 1787 and 1868. See where they were imprisoned and learn how their forced labor helped to build a new British colony.

## Lone Pine Koala Sanctuary, Queensland

Cuddle a koala, hand-feed kangaroos, and see some amazing Australian animals like the echidna and the duckbill platypus.

# Topic Tools

You can use these topic tools for your school projects. Trace the map onto a sheet of paper, using the thick black outline to guide you.

The Australian flag has a small **Union Jack** on it to show its links with the United Kingdom. Copy the flag design and then color in your picture. Make sure you use the right colors!

N

Canberra ◼

# Index

## Titles in the series

| | | | |
|---|---|---|---|
| Afghanistan | 978 1 4329 5195 5 | Japan | 978 1 4329 6102 2 |
| Algeria | 978 1 4329 6093 3 | Latvia | 978 1 4329 5211 2 |
| Australia | 978 1 4329 6094 0 | Liberia | 978 1 4329 6103 9 |
| Brazil | 978 1 4329 5196 2 | Libya | 978 1 4329 6104 6 |
| Canada | 978 1 4329 6095 7 | Lithuania | 978 1 4329 5212 9 |
| Chile | 978 1 4329 5197 9 | Mexico | 978 1 4329 5213 6 |
| China | 978 1 4329 6096 4 | Morocco | 978 1 4329 6105 3 |
| Costa Rica | 978 1 4329 5198 6 | New Zealand | 978 1 4329 6106 0 |
| Cuba | 978 1 4329 5199 3 | North Korea | 978 1 4329 6107 7 |
| Czech Republic | 978 1 4329 5200 6 | Pakistan | 978 1 4329 5214 3 |
| Egypt | 978 1 4329 6097 1 | Philippines | 978 1 4329 6108 4 |
| England | 978 1 4329 5201 3 | Poland | 978 1 4329 5215 0 |
| Estonia | 978 1 4329 5202 0 | Portugal | 978 1 4329 6109 1 |
| France | 978 1 4329 5203 7 | Russia | 978 1 4329 6110 7 |
| Germany | 978 1 4329 5204 4 | Scotland | 978 1 4329 5216 7 |
| Greece | 978 1 4329 6098 8 | South Africa | 978 1 4329 6112 1 |
| Haiti | 978 1 4329 5205 1 | South Korea | 978 1 4329 6113 8 |
| Hungary | 978 1 4329 5206 8 | Spain | 978 1 4329 6111 4 |
| Iceland | 978 1 4329 6099 5 | Tunisia | 978 1 4329 6114 5 |
| India | 978 1 4329 5207 5 | United States of America | 978 1 4329 6115 2 |
| Iran | 978 1 4329 5208 2 | Vietnam | 978 1 4329 6116 9 |
| Iraq | 978 1 4329 5209 9 | Wales | 978 1 4329 5217 4 |
| Ireland | 978 1 4329 6100 8 | Yemen | 978 1 4329 5218 1 |
| Israel | 978 1 4329 6101 5 | | |
| Italy | 978 1 4329 5210 5 | | |